Spiral Review Practice Book

Progress in Mathematics

SADLIER-OXFORD

Sadlier-Oxford
A Division of William H. Sadlier, Inc.

TABLE OF CONTENTS
Grade 1

1-1　Write One and Two

Ring how many.

Student textbook pages

See pp. 3–5.

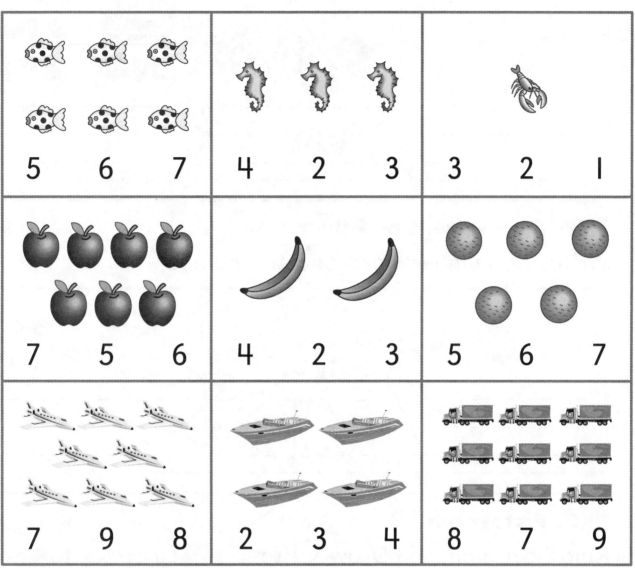

5　6　7	4　2　3	3　2　1
7　5　6	4　2　3	5　6　7
7　9　8	2　3　4	8　7　9

1-2　Write Three and Four

Write the number word and the number.

Student textbook pages

See pp. 19–20.

1

1-3 Write Five and Zero

Student textbook pages

See pp. 21–22.

Write the number word and the number.

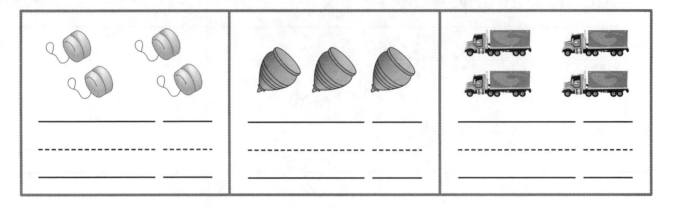

_____ _____

- - - - - - - - - - - - - - - - - - - - -

_____ _____

1-4 One More, One Fewer

Student textbook pages

See pp. 23–24.

Write the number word and the number.

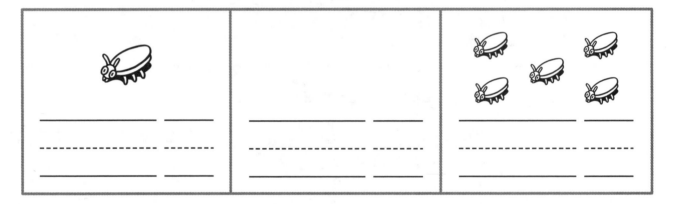

_____ _____

- - - - - - - - - - - - - - - - - - - - -

_____ _____

1-5 Pictograph

Student textbook pages

See pp. 25–26.

Ring how many in the group.	Draw ◯ to show one more.	Draw ◯ to show one fewer.
1. 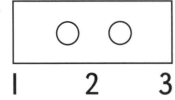 2 3 4		
2. 1 2 3		

Name _____ Date _____

Use these tallies to make a pictograph.

Student textbook pages

See pp. 27–28.

5   4   3   2   I

Draw I ☺ for each tally.

My Art Things					
🖊					
🎨					
🖌					
📦					
✂					

Student textbook pages

See pp. 29–30.

Write the number word and the number.

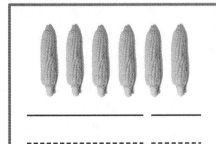 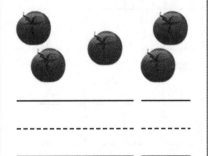 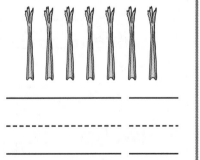

_____   _____   _____

- - - - - - - - - - - - - - - -   - - - - - - - - - - - - - - - -   - - - - - - - - - - - - - - - -

_____   _____   _____

1-8 Write Ten

Write the number word and the number.

1-9 Write Eleven and Twelve

Write the number word and the number.

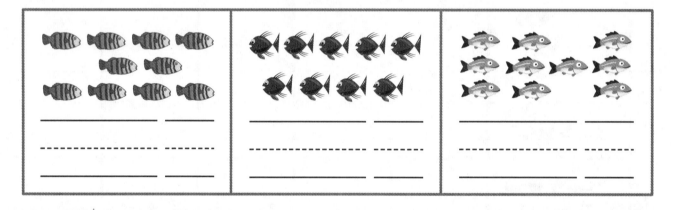

1-10 Zero to Twelve

Write the number. Draw to show the number.

eleven _____ _____

twelve _____ _____

Use ● and a ⬚. Write the missing numbers.

12 ● is ____ more than 10 ●.

1-11 Order 0–12

Student textbook pages

See pp. 37–38.

Write and draw each number.
Complete the pattern.

zero	0	
one	1	○
two		○△
three		○△○
four		○△○△
five		○△○△○
six		○△○△○△
seven		○△○△○△
eight		○△○△○△
nine		○△○△○△
ten		○△○△○△
eleven		○△○△○△
twelve		○△○△○△

I-12 Counting on a Number Line

Student textbook pages

See pp. 39–40.

Write the missing numbers.

1. ___, 1, ___, 3, ___, 5, ___, 7, ___, 9, ___, 11, ___

2. 0, 1, ___, ___, 4, 5, ___, ___, 8, 9, ___, ___, 12

3. ___, 1, 2, ___, 4, 5, ___, 7, 8, ___, 10, 11, ___

I-13 Counting Back

Student textbook pages

See pp. 41–42.

Write the missing numbers.

1.

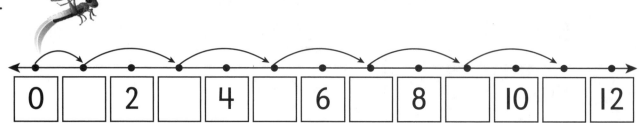

2.

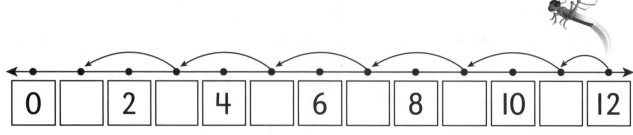

3.

1-14 Before, After, Between

Student textbook pages

See p. 43.

Count back by 1. Write the missing numbers.

1.

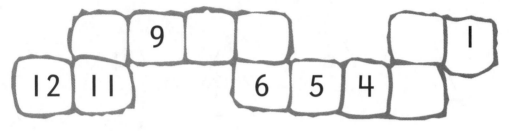

12   7 6 5
11 10   8   2 1   0

2.
9   1
12 11   6 5 4

3.
12   7
11 10 9   4 3 2   0

1-15 Compare

Student textbook pages

See p. 44.

What number comes just before?

___, 6   ___, 12   ___, 8   ___, 10

___, 1   ___, 7   ___, 4   ___, 3

What number comes just after?

2, ___   5, ___   10, ___   4, ___

8, ___   1, ___   6, ___   3, ___

What number comes between?

6, ___, 8   1, ___, 3   10, ___, 12   4, ___, 6

2, ___, 4   5, ___, 7   9, ___, 11   3, ___, 5

1-16 Odd and Even

Student textbook pages

See p. 45.

Color the numbers greater than 4.

Color the numbers less than 7.

 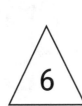  

1-17 Ordinals

Student textbook pages

See p. 46.

Draw to make pairs and leftovers.
Ring odd or even.

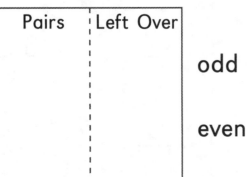

8 ●		
Pairs	Left Over	odd
		even

9 ●		
Pairs	Left Over	odd
		even

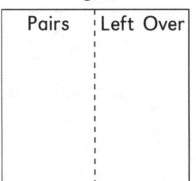

5 ●		
Pairs	Left Over	odd
		even

6 ●		
Pairs	Left Over	odd
		even

Name _____ Date _____

1-18 Problem Solving: Find a Pattern

Student textbook pages

first   second   third   fourth   fifth

tenth   ninth   eighth   seventh   sixth

Ring the correct place of each animal.

See p. 47.

third
fourth
fifth

eighth
ninth
tenth

seventh
eighth
sixth

first
fourth
seventh

ninth
second
tenth

sixth
third
first

tenth
third
second

seventh
sixth
ninth

third
seventh
second

2-1 Understanding Addition

Student textbook pages

Read ⟶ Think ⟶ Write

What comes next in the pattern?

See pp. 49–50.

Algebra 1.

3 ___ ___ ___ ___ ___

Write the number of hops.

See pp. 41–42.

2.

0 1 2 3 4 5 6 7 8 9 10 11 12

____ hops to the 🍁.   ____ more hops to the 🌼.

Write the number word and the number.

See pp. 19–20.

3.

_____ __   _____ __   _____ __

2-2 Addition Sentences

Student textbook pages

Color the tiles. Tell how many altogether.

See pp. 61–62.

1.

____ ▨ and ____ ▨

equals ____ in all.

Ring how many ●.

Draw one more ●.

See pp. 25–26.

2.   1 2 3 4 5

____

2-3 Sums of 4

Add. Fill in each addition sentence.

Student textbook pages

See pp. 63–64.

Algebra ✓

1.     2.

2 + 4 = ___   ___ + ___ = ___

Use . Write how many cents in all.

See pp. 61–62.

3.

____¢ and ____¢

equals ____¢ in all.

Write the number word and the number.

See pp. 21–22.

4.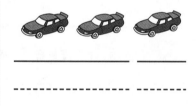

_____ ____ | _____ ____ | _____ ____

-------------------- | -------------------- | --------------------

_____ ____ | _____ ____ | _____ ____

2-4 Sums of 5

Add.

Student textbook pages

See pp. 65–66.

1.
$$\begin{array}{r} 3 \\ +0 \\ \hline \end{array}$$
2. 
$$\begin{array}{r} 2 \\ +1 \\ \hline \end{array}$$

What comes next in the pattern?

See pp. 49–50.

Algebra ✓ 3.   △   △△   △△   △   △
         △   △   △   △△   △   △

____   ____   ____   ____   ____   ____

2-5 **Sums of 6**

Student textbook pages

See pp. 67–68.

Add.

1. $3 + 2 =$ ___   2. $5 + 0 =$ ___

3. $1 + 4 =$ ___   4. $2 + 3 =$ ___

Draw 1 more . Then write how many.

See pp. 29–30.

5.   ___

Draw each group. Write the number.

See pp. 37–38.

6. six △ and eight ☐

2-6 **Change the Order**

Student textbook pages

See pp. 69–70.

Find the sum.

1. $2 + 4 =$ ___ $6 + 0 =$ ___ $3 + 3 =$ ___

Draw to make pairs and leftovers.
Ring odd or even.

See p. 46.

2.

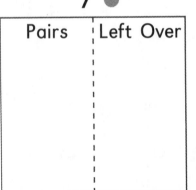

Pairs	Left Over

7 ●   odd

even

Pairs	Left Over

8 ●   odd

even

2-7 Addition Patterns

Student textbook pages

See pp. 71–72.

Add. Change the order. Draw to check.

 Algebra

1. $\begin{array}{r} 2 \\ +3 \\ \hline \end{array}$ ●● ●●● $\begin{array}{r} 3 \\ + \\ \hline \end{array}$

2. $\begin{array}{r} 1 \\ +4 \\ \hline \end{array}$ ● ●● ●● $\begin{array}{r} \\ + \\ \hline \end{array}$

Find the sum.

See pp. 69–70.

3. $\begin{array}{r} 5 \\ +1 \\ \hline \end{array}$ $\begin{array}{r} 4 \\ +2 \\ \hline \end{array}$ $\begin{array}{r} 3 \\ +3 \\ \hline \end{array}$ $\begin{array}{r} 2 \\ +4 \\ \hline \end{array}$ $\begin{array}{r} 1 \\ +5 \\ \hline \end{array}$

4. $\begin{array}{r} 0 \\ +5 \\ \hline \end{array}$ $\begin{array}{r} 1 \\ +4 \\ \hline \end{array}$ $\begin{array}{r} 2 \\ +3 \\ \hline \end{array}$ $\begin{array}{r} 3 \\ +2 \\ \hline \end{array}$ $\begin{array}{r} 4 \\ +1 \\ \hline \end{array}$

What number comes just before?

See p. 44.

5. ___, 7   ___, 2   ___, 8   ___, 11

What number comes just after?

6. 9, ___   3, ___   8, ___   2, ___

What number comes between?

7. 5, ___, 7   9, ___, 11   7, ___, 9

Student textbook pages

See p. 74.

Add. Look for the pattern.

Algebra ✓ 1.

5	4	3	2	1
+1	+1	+1	+1	+1

Sort the flowers to make a picture graph.

See pp. 27–28.

Color 1 picture for each flower. Then write the number.

2.

four	🌼	🌼	🌼	🌼	
three	🌷	🌷	🌷	🌷	
two	🌸	🌸	🌸	🌸	
one	🌼	🌼	🌼	🌼	

Use the picture graph above.

3. Ring the flower that is one more than .

Write the missing number word.

See pp. 39–40.

4. five, _____, seven   5. nine, _____, eleven

3-1 Understanding Subtraction

Student textbook pages

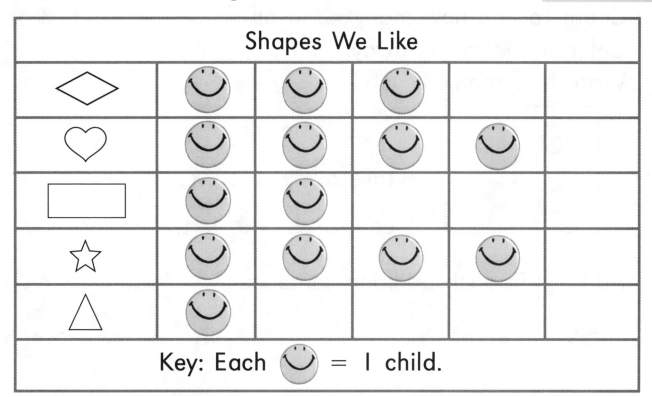

Shapes We Like

Key: Each ☺ = 1 child.

Ring your choice.

See pp. 77–78.

1. Do more 🯅 like ♡ than ☆?   Yes or   No

Ring how many ●.   Draw one fewer ●.

See pp. 25–26.

Algebra 2.   1 2 3 4 5

Write the number word and the number.

See pp. 23–24.

3.

   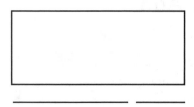

_____ ____   _____ ____   _____ ____

- - - - - - - - - ---   - - - - - - - - - ---   - - - - - - - - - ---

3-2 Subtraction Symbols

Student textbook pages

See pp. 89–90.

Count to find how many in all.
Color the taken away.
Write how many left.

1.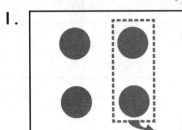

_____  in all,

take away _____ ,

equals _____ left.

Add. Fill in each addition sentence.

See pp. 63–64.

 Algebra

2.

3.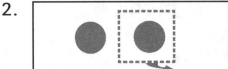

_____ + _____ = _____   _____ + _____ = _____

3-3 Subtract from 4

Student textbook pages

See pp. 91–92.

Subtract.

1.

2.

3 − 2 = _____   2 − 1 = _____

Add.

See pp. 65–66.

3.

$$\begin{array}{r} 3 \\ +1 \\ \hline \end{array}$$

4.

$$\begin{array}{r} 2 \\ +2 \\ \hline \end{array}$$

16

3-4 Subtract from 5

Student textbook pages

See pp. 93–94.

Subtract.

1.

$$\begin{array}{r} 4 \\ -3 \\ \hline \end{array}$$

2.

$$\begin{array}{r} 4 \\ -4 \\ \hline \end{array}$$

Add.

See pp. 67–68.

3. $1 + 4 =$ ___ $3 + 2 =$ ___ $0 + 5 =$ ___

3-5 Subtract from 6

Student textbook pages

See pp. 95–96.

Subtract.

1. $5 - 1 =$ ___ $5 - 4 =$ ___ $5 - 2 =$ ___

Add. Change the order. Draw to check.

See p. 71.

Algebra ✓ 2.
$$\begin{array}{r} 3 \\ +2 \\ \hline \end{array}$$
●●●
●●
$$\begin{array}{r} 2 \\ + \\ \hline \end{array}$$

3.
$$\begin{array}{r} 2 \\ +4 \\ \hline \end{array}$$
●●
●●
●●
$$\begin{array}{r} \\ + \\ \hline \end{array}$$

4.
$$\begin{array}{r} 1 \\ +4 \\ \hline \end{array}$$
●
●●
●●
$$\begin{array}{r} \\ + \\ \hline \end{array}$$

5.
$$\begin{array}{r} 3 \\ +0 \\ \hline \end{array}$$
●●●
$$\begin{array}{r} \\ + \\ \hline \end{array}$$

3-6 Subtraction Patterns

Subtract.

Student textbook pages

See pp. 97–98.

1.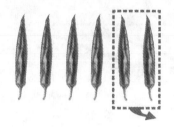

$6 - 2 = $ _____

2.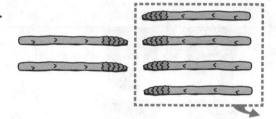

$6 - 4 = $ _____

What number comes between?

See p. 44.

3. 3, ___, 5   7, ___, 9   0, ___, 2

4. 6, ___, 8   10, ___, 12   4, ___, 6

3-7 Relate Addition and Subtraction

Subtract. Look for patterns.

Student textbook pages

See p. 100.

Algebra ✓

1.

1	2	3	4	5	6
−0	−0	−0	−0	−0	−0

Look at the bar graph.

See pp. 77–78.

Kind	Toys Sold					
🪁	▨	▨	▨	▨		
🪀	▨	▨	▨	▨	▨	
🚗	▨	▨	▨	▨		
✈	▨	▨	▨			
	0	1	2	3	4	5	6

Ring your choice.

2. Did the store sell more or ?

3-8 Zero in Facts

Student textbook pages

 Write the related number sentences.

See p. 101.

1. $4 + 1 = $ _____

5 $-$ _____ $= $ _____

2. $3 + 2 = $ _____

_____ $-$ _____ $= $ _____

Add.

See pp. 65–66.

3.
$$\begin{array}{r} 4 \\ +0 \\ \hline \end{array}$$

4.
$$\begin{array}{r} 2 \\ +1 \\ \hline \end{array}$$

5. Count back by 1. Write the missing numbers.

See p. 43.

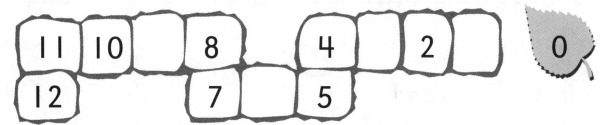

| 11 | 10 | | 8 | | 4 | | 2 | | 0 |
| 12 | | 7 | | 5 | | | | |

Write the subtraction story. Use .

See pp. 89–90.

6.

In all _____¢.

Take away _____¢ equals

_____¢ left.

Student textbook pages

Algebra Write the number sentence. Use ■.

See p. 102.

1. 4 ■ in all. Take away 0. How many ■ left?

2. 6 ■ in all. Take away all. How many ■ left?

___ – ___ = ___   ___ – ___ = ___

Algebra

Ring how many in the group.

3.

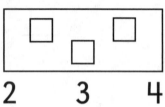

2   3   4

Draw ☐ to show one more.

Draw ☐ to show one fewer.

See pp. 25–26.

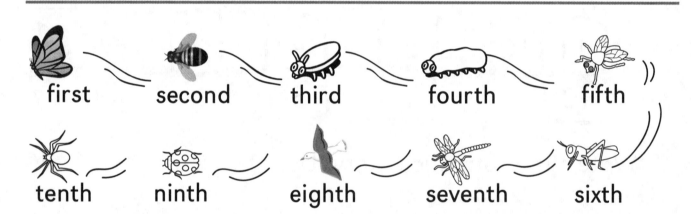

first   second   third   fourth   fifth

tenth   ninth   eighth   seventh   sixth

4. Ring the correct place of each animal.

See pp. 47–48.

fourth   eighth   sixth

fifth   ninth   seventh

sixth   tenth   eighth

Name _____ Date _____

4-1 Sums of 7

Student textbook pages

Read ⟶ Model ⟶ Ring ⟶ Write   See pp. 103–104.

 Algebra

1. Sam has 4 🎈.
He buys 2 more.
How many 🎈 in all?

sum   difference

_____

____ 🎈 in all.

Write the number word and the number.   See pp. 29–30.

2.

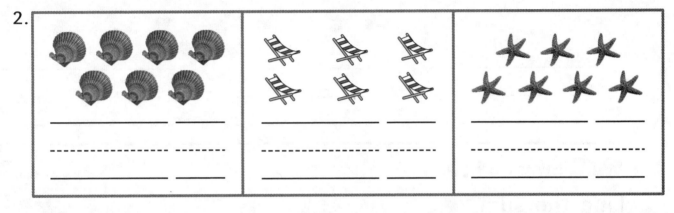

4-2 Sums of 8

Student textbook pages

Color 🖍 red and write the number sentence.   See pp. 117–118.

Algebra

1.

$$6 + \underline{} = \underline{}$$

part gray   part red   in all

2.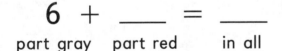

$$\underline{} + \underline{} = \underline{}$$

part gray   part red   in all

3. Write the number that is one fewer.   See pp. 31–32.

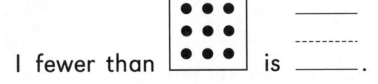

I fewer than [⠿] is ____ .

4-3 Sums of 9

Find the sum.

Student textbook pages

See pp. 119–120.

1.

$5 + 3 =$ ___

2.

$3 + 5 =$ ___

Write the number word and the number.

See pp. 33–34.

3.

_____ _____

\- - - - - - - - - - - - - - - - - -

_____ _____

4-4 Sums of 10

Find the sum.

Student textbook pages

See pp. 121–122.

1.

$8 + 1 =$ ___

2.

$1 + 8 =$ ___

Write how many.

See pp. 39–40.

3. ____   ____   ____   ____

Subtract. Fill in the subtraction sentence.

See pp. 91–92.

Algebra ✓

4.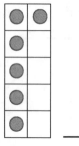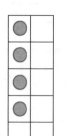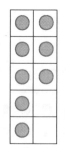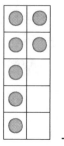

___ − ___ = ___

4-5 Sums of 11

Student textbook pages

See pp. 123–124.

Fill in the 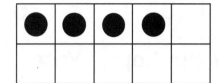. Add.

1.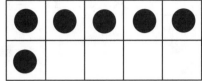

$6 + 4 =$ ___

2.

$4 + 6 =$ ___

Write the number word. Draw ● to show the number. See pp. 35–36.

3.

_____

_ _ _ _ _ _ _ _ _ _ _ _

12 _____

What comes next in the pattern? See pp. 49–50.

Algebra 4.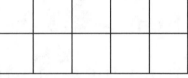

10, ___, ___, ___, ____

4-6 Sums of 12

Student textbook pages

See pp. 125–126.

Find the sum.

1.

$3 + 8 =$ ___

2.

$8 + 3 =$ ___

Subtract. See pp. 93–94.

3.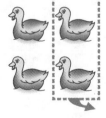

$\begin{array}{r} 4 \\ -2 \\ \hline \end{array}$

4.

$\begin{array}{r} 4 \\ -4 \\ \hline \end{array}$

Student textbook pages

See pp. 127–128.

4-7 Number-Line Addition

Find the sum.

1. $4 + 8 =$ ___ $6 + 5 =$ ___ $8 + 4 =$ ___

Draw the hops. Write the number.

See pp. 41–42.

2.

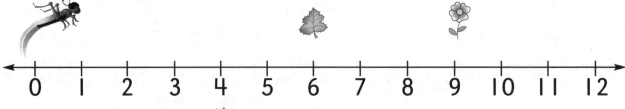

___ hops from 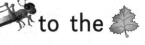 to the 🍂.

___ hops from the 🍂 to the 🌸.

Subtract. Write the next fact.

See p. 100.

 3.

6	5	4	3	2	1
−0	−0	−0	−0	−0	−0

4-8 Add: Use Patterns

Student textbook pages

See pp. 129–130.

Show how you count on to add. Write the sum.

1.

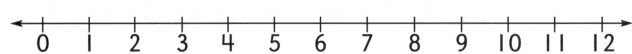

$9 + 3 =$ ___

Subtract.

See pp. 95–96.

2. $5 - 4 =$ ___ $5 - 5 =$ ___ $5 - 2 =$ ___

4-9 Doubles and Near Doubles

Add. Look for the pattern.
Write the next addition sentence.

Student textbook pages

See pp. 131–132.

1. $4 + 3 =$ ___

    $5 + 3 =$ ___

    $6 + 3 =$ ___

    ___ $+$ ___ $=$ ___

2. $8 + 1 =$ ___

    $7 + 2 =$ ___

    $6 + 3 =$ ___

    ___ $+$ ___ $=$ ___

Ring how many
in the group.

Draw ▲ to show
one more.

See pp. 25–26.

3.

3   4   5

Write the missing numbers.

See pp. 39–40.

4. ___, 1, 2, ___, 4, ___, ___, 7, 8, ___, 10, ___, ___

4-10 Adding Three Numbers

Draw the part joined in each doubles fact.
Complete the addition sentence.

Student textbook pages

See pp. 133–134.

1.

___ $+$ ___ $=$ ___

2.

___ $+$ ___ $=$ ___

Find the difference.

See pp. 97–98.

3. $6 - 0 =$ ___ $6 - 2 =$ ___ $6 - 5 =$ ___

Find the sum. Ring the numbers you add first.

Student textbook pages
See pp. 135–136.

 1. 2 + 2 + 3 = ___   2. 1 + 4 + 4 = ___

___ + ___ = ___   ___ + ___ = ___

Add.

See pp. 67–68.

3. 1 + 4 = ___   5 + 0 = ___   2 + 3 = ___

4-12 Addition Strategies

Student textbook pages
See pp. 137–138.

Write an addition sentence for the ·——→ .

1.
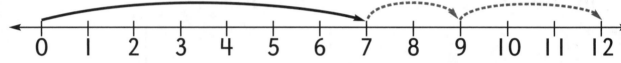

___ + ___ + ___ = ___

Complete the doubles fact.

See pp. 69–70,
133–134.

2.
   2¢
  +2¢
  ——

3.
   3¢
  +3¢
  ——

Find the sum.

See pp. 69–70.

4.   5¢   3¢   4¢   1¢   2¢
    +1¢   +2¢   +0¢   +2¢   +4¢
    ——   ——   ——   ——   ——

4-14 Problem Solving: Ask a Question

Student textbook pages

See pp. 141–142.

Write the missing output numbers.

1.

| Input | I more | Output |

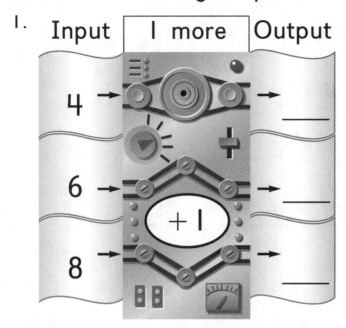

4 → _____

6 → _____

+ 1

8 → _____

Read → Model → Ring → Write

Algebra ✓

Solve.

See pp. 103–104.

2. Josh finds 4 🐞.
   He finds 2 more.
   How many 🐞 in all?

   sum   difference

   ___ ___ ___ = ___

   ___ 🐞 in all.

3. You see 5 🦋.
   3 fly away.
   How many 🦋 are left?

   sum   difference

   ___ ___ ___ = ___

   ___ 🦋 are left.

Complete the related number sentences.

See p. 101.

Algebra ✓ 4. 3 + 2 = ___   5 − ___ = ___

5-1 Other Names: Sums and Differences

Student textbook pages
See pp. 143–144.

Choose the question. Write the number sentence.

1. Siva finds 7 .
   Then she finds 3 more.

   ○ How many in all?

   ○ How many are left?

   ___ ○ ___ = ___

Add.

See pp. 117–118.

2. △ △ △ △
   △ △   △

   4 + 3 = ___

3. △ △ △ △
    △   △ △

   3 + 4 = ___

5-2 Subtract from 7

Student textbook pages

Write other names for 7.

See pp. 155–156.

Algebra 1.

 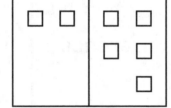 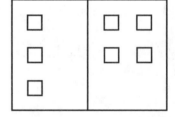

1 + ___ = ___ + ___ = ___ + ___

Add.

See pp. 65–66.

2.
$$\begin{array}{cccccc} 2 & 0 & 1 & 4 & 3 & 1 \\ +2 & +3 & +2 & +0 & +1 & +1 \\ \hline \end{array}$$

5-3 Subtract from 8

Subtract. Tell how many are left.

Student textbook pages

See pp. 157–158.

1.

$$7 - 5 = \underline{\quad}$$

2.

$$7 - 2 = \underline{\quad}$$

Look at the bar graph.

See pp. 77–78.

Kind	Things Seen At the Beach					
	▨	▨	▨	▨	▨	
	▨	▨	▨			
●	▨	▨	▨	▨		
	0	1	2	3	4	5	6

3. Ring your choice.
   Were most of the things seen ● or ⧗ ?

5-4 Subtract from 9

Ring the part taken away. Subtract.

Student textbook pages

See pp. 159–160.

1.

2.

$$8 - 2 = \underline{\quad} \qquad 8 - 6 = \underline{\quad}$$

Add. Ring sums less than 9.

See pp. 121–122.

3.
$$\begin{array}{cccccc} 6 & 2 & 9 & 5 & 6 & 1 \\ +3 & +5 & +0 & +4 & +2 & +8 \end{array}$$

Student textbook pages

See pp. 161–162.

Find the difference.

1.

$$9 - 7 = \rule{1.5cm}{0.4pt}$$

2.

$$9 - 2 = \rule{1.5cm}{0.4pt}$$

Add. Fill in each addition sentence.

See pp. 63–64.

Algebra ✓ 3.

$$\rule{1cm}{0.4pt} + \rule{1cm}{0.4pt} = \rule{1cm}{0.4pt}$$

4.

$$\rule{1cm}{0.4pt} + \rule{1cm}{0.4pt} = \rule{1cm}{0.4pt}$$

Student textbook pages

See pp. 163–164.

Draw ● to show the part taken away.
Find the difference.

1.

♥	♥	♥	♥	

$$10 - 6 = \rule{1.5cm}{0.4pt}$$

2.

♥	♥	♥	♥	♥
♥				

$$10 - 4 = \rule{1.5cm}{0.4pt}$$

Algebra ✓ 3. Write what comes next in the pattern.

See pp. 49–50.

$$4, \quad 2, \quad 6, \quad \rule{1cm}{0.4pt}, \quad \rule{1cm}{0.4pt}, \quad \rule{1cm}{0.4pt}$$

Name _____ Date _____

5-7 Subtract from 12

Student textbook pages
See pp. 165–166.

Find the difference. Ring the ⭐ being taken away.

1.

$$11 - 7 = \underline{\quad}$$ $$11 - \underline{\quad} = \underline{\quad}$$

Subtract. Fill in each subtraction sentence.

See pp. 91–92.

2.

3.

$$\underline{\quad} - \underline{\quad} = \underline{\quad}$$ $$\underline{\quad} - \underline{\quad} = \underline{\quad}$$

5-8 Number-Line Subtraction

Student textbook pages
See pp. 167–168.

Subtract. Ring the part taken away.

1.

$$12 - 5 = \underline{\quad}$$ $$12 - 7 = \underline{\quad}$$

Write the doubles fact. Draw one more.
Write the new addition fact.

See pp. 133–134.

Algebra ✓ 2. 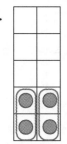 $\underline{\quad} + \underline{\quad}$ $\underline{\quad} + \underline{\quad}$

3. 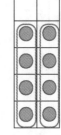 $\underline{\quad} + \underline{\quad}$ $\underline{\quad} + \underline{\quad}$

5-9 Subtract: Use Patterns

Student textbook pages

See pp. 169–170.

Subtract. Show how you count back.

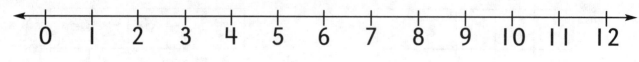

1. 11 – 4 = ___

Subtract. Write the next fact.

See p. 100.

Algebra ✓ 2.

6	5	4	3	2	1
–1	–1	–1	–1	–1	–1

Subtract.

See pp. 93–94.

Algebra ✓

3. 4 – 1 = ___   4 – 4 = ___   3 – 1 = ___

5-10 Subtraction Strategies

Student textbook pages

See pp. 171–172.

Subtract. Look for the pattern.
Write the next number sentence.

Algebra ✓ 1.

12 – 3 = ___   2.   12 – 7 = ___

10 – 3 = ___   11 – 6 = ___

8 – 3 = ___   10 – 5 = ___

___ – ___ = ___   ___ – ___ = ___

Fill in the ●. Add.

See pp. 123–124.

3.
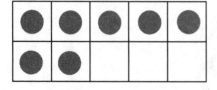

7 + 3 = ___

4.
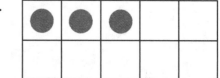

3 + 7 = ___

5-11 Check by Adding

Student textbook pages

Find the difference. Use a strategy you have learned. See p. 173.

1.
$$
\begin{array}{r} 12 \\ -\ 7 \\ \hline \end{array}
\qquad
\begin{array}{r} 11 \\ -\ 3 \\ \hline \end{array}
\qquad
\begin{array}{r} 12 \\ -\ 8 \\ \hline \end{array}
\qquad
\begin{array}{r} 11¢ \\ -\ 4¢ \\ \hline \end{array}
\qquad
\begin{array}{r} 10¢ \\ -\ 4¢ \\ \hline \end{array}
$$

Write the related number sentences. See p. 101.

 2. $3 + 4 =$ ___

$7 -$ ___ $=$ ___

3. $6 + 2 =$ ___

$8 -$ ___ $=$ ___

 Read ⟶ Model ⟶ Ring ⟶ Write See pp. 103–104.

 1. Tanya has 3 .
She gets 1 more.
How many does
Tanya have now?

sum   difference

___

___ in all.

5-12 Fact Families

Student textbook pages

Subtract. Check by adding. See pp. 175–176.

1.
$$
\begin{array}{r} 10 \\ -\ 3 \\ \hline \end{array}
\ +
\qquad
\begin{array}{r} 12 \\ -\ 7 \\ \hline \end{array}
\ +
\qquad
\begin{array}{r} 11 \\ -\ 6 \\ \hline \end{array}
\ +
$$

Write the addition sentence for the ⟶ . See pp. 129–130.

2.

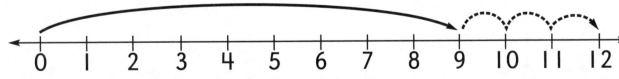

0 1 2 3 4 5 6 7 8 9 10 11 12

___ $+$ ___ $=$ ___

Student textbook pages

Solve. Write the fact families.

See pp. 177–178.

Algebra 1.

2.

6 + 2 = ___   4 + 3 = ___

___ ◯ ___ = ___   ___ ◯ ___ = ___

___ ◯ ___ = ___   ___ ◯ ___ = ___

___ ◯ ___ = ___   ___ ◯ ___ = ___

Find the sum. Use a strategy you have learned.

See p. 139.

3.
$$\begin{array}{cccccc}
9 & 6 & 9 & 4 & 7¢ & 8¢ \\
+2 & +4 & +1 & +6 & +5¢ & +4¢ \\
\hline
 & & & & ¢ & ¢
\end{array}$$

6-1 Numbers 10–19

Student textbook pages

Read → Draw → Think → Write   *See pp. 179–180.*

Algebra ✓ 1. Sam made 8 🧁

Joan made 5 🧁

Who made fewer 🧁?

How many fewer?

Sam	
Joan	

___ ◯ ___ = ___   _____ made ___ fewer 🧁.

Subtract.   *See pp. 95–96.*

2. $5 - 4 =$ ___ $4 - 2 =$ ___ $5 - 0 =$ ___

6-2 Ten to Nineteen

Student textbook pages

See pp. 193–194.

Write how many.

1.

fifteen

___ ten ___ ones

___ + ___   ___

2.

seventeen

___ ten ___ ones

___ + ___   ___

What number comes just after?   *See p. 44.*

3. 7, ___   10, ___   5, ___   9, ___

Add. Ring facts that belong.   *See pp. 119–120.*

4.
$$\boxed{8}$$
$$\begin{array}{cccccc} 7 & 2 & 3 & 4 & 6 & 5 \\ +1 & +4 & +5 & +4 & +2 & +2 \end{array}$$

Student textbook pages

See pp. 195–196.

Write the number and number word.
Color the number.

1. 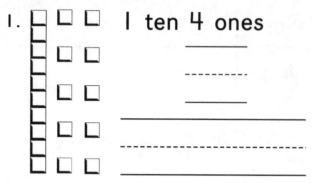 I ten 4 ones

2. 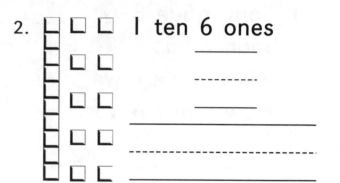 I ten 6 ones

Add.

See pp. 125–126.

3.
$$7 + 4$$ $$5 + 4$$ $$3 + 5$$ $$3 + 8$$ $$9 + 2$$ $$5 + 5$$

6-4 **Numbers 20–39**

Student textbook pages

See pp. 197–198.

Write how many tens.
Write the number and number word.

1. 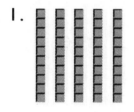 _____ tens _____

2. 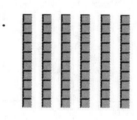 _____ tens _____

Subtract.

See pp. 97–98.

3.
$$5¢ - 1¢ = \_\_¢$$ $$6¢ - 2¢ = \_\_¢$$ $$6¢ - 0¢ = \_\_¢$$ $$4¢ - 2¢ = \_\_¢$$ $$6¢ - 3¢ = \_\_¢$$

Name _____   Date _____

Name _____   Date _____

6-5 Numbers 40–59

Student textbook pages
See pp. 199–200.

Write how many.

1.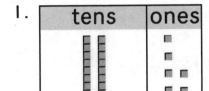

____ tens ____ ones

Subtract. Write the next fact.

See pp. 100, 163–164.

Algebra ✓ 2.

$$10 \\ -\ 2$$ $$8 \\ -\ 2$$ $$6 \\ -\ 2$$ $$4 \\ -\ $$ $$\\ -\ $$

6-6 Numbers through 59

Student textbook pages
See pp. 201–202.

Write how many.

1.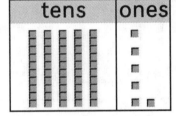

2.

____ tens ____ ones   ____ tens ____ ones

Algebra ✓ 3. Write other names for 8.

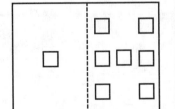  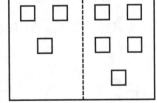

$$1 + \_\_ = \_\_ + \_\_ = \_\_ + \_\_ = \_\_ + \_\_$$

Copyright © by William H. Sadlier, Inc. All rights reserved.

37

6-7 Numbers 60–79

Student textbook pages

See pp. 203–204.

Write the place value and the number.

1. twenty-four ____

   ____ tens ____ ones

2. fifty-seven ____

   ____ tens ____ ones

Add.

See pp. 127–128.

3.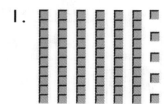

7	6	8	4	9	5
+5	+6	+3	+8	+3	+5

6-8 Numbers 80–99

Student textbook pages

See pp. 205–206.

Write how many.

1.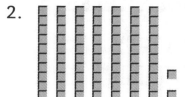

   ____ tens ____ ones

   _____ _____

   _____ _____

   _____ _____

2.

   ____ tens ____ ones

   _____ _____

   _____ _____

   _____ _____

Ring the number.

See pp. 203–204.

3. Which has more tens? 24 42

4. Which has more ones? 24 42

Find the sum. Complete the pattern.

See pp. 131–132.

Algebra

5.
4	4	4	4	
+0	+2	+4	+	+

6-9 Numbers to 100

Write how many.

Student textbook pages

See pp. 207–208.

1.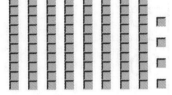

____ tens ____ ones

_____   _____

- - - - - -   - - - - - - - - - - - - -

_____   _____

2.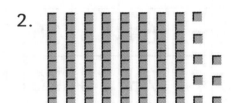

____ tens ____ ones

_____   _____

- - - - - -   - - - - - - - - - - - - -

_____   _____

| Read | → | Model | → | Ring | → | Write |

See pp. 103–104.

Algebra ✓ 3. Leslie catches 7 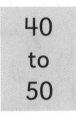.
3 hop away.
How many 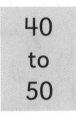 are left?

sum   difference

____

____ are left.

6-10 Hundred Chart Patterns

Write the missing numbers.

Student textbook pages

See pp. 209–210.

Algebra ✓ 1.

| 40 to 50 |

40   42   44   46   48   50

____ ____ ____ ____ ____

Write the related number sentences.

See p. 101.

Algebra ✓ 2. $3 + 6 =$ ____

$9 -$ ____ $=$ ____

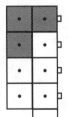

3. $5 + 3 =$ ____

$8 -$ ____ $=$ ____

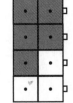

Student textbook pages

See pp. 211–212.

6-11 Count On: Number After

51	52	53	54	55	56	57	58	59	60
61	62	63	64	65	66	67	68	69	70
71	72	73	74	75	76	77	78	79	80
81	82	83	84	85	86	87	88	89	90
91	92	93	94	95	96	97	98	99	100

Find the pattern. Write the missing numbers.

 Algebra

1. 69, 70, 71, ___, ___   2. 52, 62, 72, ___, ___

Subtract.

See pp. 157–158.

3.
$$\begin{array}{r} 7 \\ -2 \\ \hline \end{array} \qquad \begin{array}{r} 7 \\ -5 \\ \hline \end{array} \qquad \begin{array}{r} 6 \\ -1 \\ \hline \end{array} \qquad \begin{array}{r} 7 \\ -4 \\ \hline \end{array} \qquad \begin{array}{r} 6 \\ -2 \\ \hline \end{array}$$

6-12 Count Back: Number Before

Student textbook pages

See pp. 213–214.

Write the number that comes just after.

 Algebra 1.

2.

Add.

See pp. 121–122.

3.
$$\begin{array}{r} 7 \\ +2 \\ \hline \end{array} \qquad \begin{array}{r} 5 \\ +4 \\ \hline \end{array} \qquad \begin{array}{r} 3 \\ +5 \\ \hline \end{array} \qquad \begin{array}{r} 6 \\ +3 \\ \hline \end{array} \qquad \begin{array}{r} 9 \\ +0 \\ \hline \end{array} \qquad \begin{array}{r} 1 \\ +6 \\ \hline \end{array}$$

6-13 Before, Between, After

Student textbook pages

See p. 214.

Write the number that comes just before.

1. ___, 45, 46   2. ___, 81, 82

See p. 44.

What number comes between?

3. 6, ___, 8   10, ___, 12   9, ___, 11

Draw the part joined in each doubles fact.
Complete the addition sentence.

See pp. 133–134.

Algebra ✓ 4.    5.

___ + ___ = ___   ___ + ___ = ___

6-14 Greater Than, Less Than

Student textbook pages

See p. 215.

Write the number that comes between.

1. **Between**   2. **Between**

before   after   before   after

61,   ___,   63   57,   ___,   59

Write how many.

See pp. 201–202,
205–206.

3. 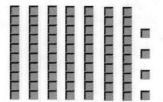   ___ tens ___ ones

___   _____

------   ------------------

___   _____

Find the sum. Use a strategy you have learned.

See p. 139.

4.   8   6   8   4   4¢
    +3   +5   +2   +6   +8¢

                                                ¢

6-15 **Count by Fives**

Student textbook pages

Write the numbers. Compare. Ring the greater.

See pp. 217–218.

 1.

tens	ones

____

____

2.

tens	ones

____

____

Subtract.

See pp. 159–160.

3.
$$8 - 6 \qquad 8 - 0 \qquad 8 - 5 \qquad 7 - 3 \qquad 8 - 8 \qquad 6 - 2$$

6-16 **Count by Twos**

Student textbook pages

See pp. 219–220.

1	2	3	4	5	6	7	8	9	10
11	12	13	14	15	16	17	18	19	20
21	22	23	24	25	26	27	28	29	30
31	32	33	34	35	36	37	38	39	40
41	42	43	44	45	46	47	48	49	50

Continue to count by 5s. Use the hundred chart.

 1. 15, 20, ____, ____, ____, ____, ____, 50

Find the sum.

See pp. 123–124.

2. $5 + 5 =$ ____ $4 + 5 =$ ____ $2 + 8 =$ ____

6-17 Equal Groups

Student textbook pages
See pp. 221–222.

Count by 2s. Write how many in all.

1. How many ?

____, ____, ____, ____, ____, ____   ____ in all.

Write how many tens.

See pp. 197–198.

Write the number and number word.

2. ____ tens ____

_____

_____

3. ____ tens ____

_____

_____

Subtract.

See pp. 161–162.

4. $9 - 5 =$ ___ $9 - 9 =$ ___ $9 - 3 =$ ___

6-18 Sharing

Student textbook pages
See pp. 223–224.

Make equal groups. Write the missing numbers.

1.

2.

____ groups of ____ = ____   ____ groups of ____ = ____

____ tens = ____   ____ fives = ____

Show how you count on to add. Write the sum.

See pp. 129–130.

Algebra ✓ 3.

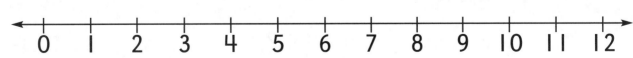

$7 + 4 =$ ___

6-19 Separating

Student textbook pages

Share. Tally. Write how many are in each group. See pp. 225–226.

1. Three share 9 .

2. Two share 14 .

[three boxes] [two boxes]

____ each ____  each

---

Make equal groups. See pp. 223–224.
Write the missing numbers.

3. [six corn/fish images in 2 rows of 3]

____ groups of 2 = ____

____ twos = ____

4. [fifteen cherries in 3 rows of 5]

____ groups of 5 = ____

____ fives = ____

Find the sum. Ring the numbers you add first. See pp. 135–136.

Algebra ✓ 5. $3 + 3 + 2 =$ ____

6. $5 + 2 + 2 =$ ____

____ + ____ = ____

____ + ____ = ____

Choose the question. Write the number sentence. See pp. 143–144.

Algebra ✓ 7. Luis sees 8 .
Then two float away.

◯ How many in all?

◯ How many are left? ____ ◯ ____ = ____

44

6-21 Problem Solving: Guess and Test

Student textbook pages

See pp. 227–228.

Ring □ to show equal groups.
Write how many equal groups.

1. I□□□□□□□□□□ 8 □
   2 in each group

   □ □ □ □ □ □ □ □ □
   □ □ □ □ □ □ □ □ □

   ____ = ____ groups of two

2. 2□□□□□□□□□□ I □
   3 in each group

   □ □ □ □ □ □ □
   □ □ □ □ □ □ □
   □ □ □ □ □ □ □

   ____ = ____ groups of three

Ring to show equal groups.
Write how many groups.

See pp. 227–228.

3. 16 shells in all
   2 in each group

   ____ = ____ groups of two

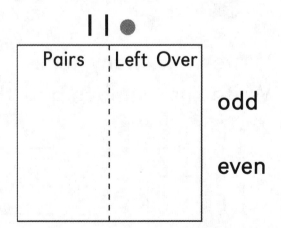

Draw to make pairs and leftovers.
Ring odd or even.

See p. 46.

4. 12 ●

Pairs	Left Over

odd

even

11 ●

Pairs	Left Over

odd

even

Subtract.

See pp. 165–166.

5. $11 - 2 =$ ____ $11 - 5 =$ ____ $11 - 7 =$ ____

7-1 Nickels

Read ──────────────→ Think → Write → Check

Student textbook pages
See pp. 231–232.

Algebra ✓

1. I am an even number greater than 15 but less than 40. What number am I?

Which numbers in the ⬡ are even? ____, ____, ____

Which of these are greater than 15? ____, ____

Which is less than 40? ____

Make equal groups. Write the missing numbers. See pp. 223–224.

2. ____ groups of 5 = ____

____ fives = ____

7-2 Dimes

Student textbook pages

Write how much. See p. 243.

1.

____ nickels = ____¢

Write how many tens. See pp. 197–198.
Write the number and the number word.

2.

____ tens ____

_____

_____

Subtract. See pp. 161–162.

3. 9 – 5 = ____   9 – 1 = ____   9 – 8 = ____

7-3 Count on by Pennies

Student textbook pages

See p. 244.

Write how much.

1.

8 dimes = ____¢

Show how you count on to add. Write the sum.

See pp. 129–130.

 2. 5 + 4 = ____

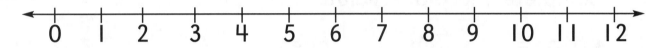

Find the sum.

See pp. 117–118.

3. 6 + 1 = ____   2 + 4 = ____   5 + 2 = ____

7-4 Quarters

Student textbook pages

See pp. 245–246.

Write how much.

1.   ____¢

Show how you count on to add. Write the sum.

See pp. 129–130.

2. 4 + 8 = ____

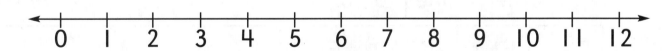

Write the subtraction sentence for the ⟵┄┄→ .

See pp. 169–170.

Algebra 3.

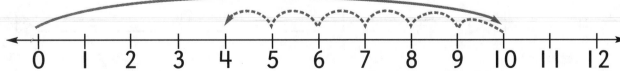

____ – ____ = ____

Count on. Write the amount.

See pp. 247–248.

1.   ____ ¢

Count by 5s. Write the missing numbers.

See pp. 219–220.

Algebra ✓ 2. ____, 25, ____, 35, ____, ____, 50, ____, 60

Complete the place value.

See pp. 207–208.

3. 83 = ____ tens ____ ones

Write how much.

See pp. 249–250.

1.   ____ ¢

Find the sum. Ring the numbers you add first.

See pp. 135–136.

Algebra ✓ 2. $5 + 3 + 2 =$ ____   3. $8 + 2 + 1 =$ ____

____ + ____ = ____   ____ + ____ = ____

Write other names for 6.

See pp. 155–156.

Algebra ✓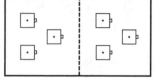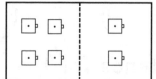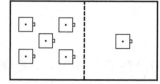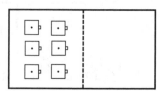

4. $3 + 3$ = ____ + ____ = ____ + ____ = ____ + ____

7-7 Trading

Student textbook pages
See pp. 251–252.

Write how much.

1.   _____¢

Write how many.

See pp. 193–194.

2. 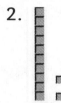 _____ ten _____ ones

_____

- - - - - - - - - - - - - - - - - - -

_____ + _____ = _____   _____

7-8 Using Money

Student textbook pages

1st Write how much.

See pp. 253–254.

2nd Match equal amounts.

1.  _____¢

2.  _____¢

3.  _____¢

4.  _____¢

Count by 5s. Write the missing numbers.

See pp. 219–220.

Algebra ✓ 5.

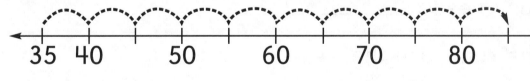

35 40 _____ 50 _____ 60 _____ 70 _____ 80 _____

_____   _____   _____   _____   _____

Write the place value and number.

See pp. 203–204.

6. fifty-six _____

_____ tens _____ ones

7. twenty-one _____

_____ tens _____ one

49

7-9 Equal Amounts

Student textbook pages

See pp. 255–256.

Write the amount. Match.

1.   ___ ¢    31¢

2.   ___ ¢    16¢

See p. 214.

Write the number that comes just before.

3. ___, 40, 41   4. ___, 71, 72   5. ___, 45, 46

7-10 Hour

Student textbook pages

See p. 257.

Trade. Complete the table.

1. Monica    ___ ___

Antony   ___ ___

Antony needs ___ _____.

See pp. 137–138.

Find the sum. Use the ↤┼┼┼┼→ .

2.

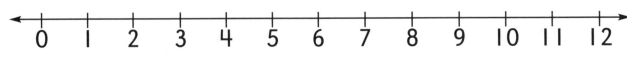

4 + 6 + 1 = ___

7-11 Half Hour

Student textbook pages

See pp. 259–260.

Write the time in 2 ways.

1.  _____ o'clock

Count by 5s. Write the missing numbers.

See pp. 219–220.

Algebra ✓

2. 0, ____, 10, 15, ____, 25, ____, ____, 40, ____, 50

Share. Tally.

See pp. 225–226.

Write how many are in each group.

3. Four share 12  .

_____ each

7-12 Time Patterns

Student textbook pages

See pp. 261–262.

Write the time in 2 ways.

1.    half past _____   :

Find the pattern. Write the missing numbers.

See pp. 211–212.

Algebra ✓

2. 38, 36, 34, ____, ____

Ring the part taken away. Subtract.

See pp. 159–160.

3.

8 – 2 = ____

7-13 Name the Time

Student textbook pages

See pp. 263–264.

Draw the time that comes next.

Algebra ✓ 1.

____ o'clock   half past ____   ____ o'clock

Solve. Write the fact family.

See pp. 177–178.

Algebra ✓ 2. $4 + 3 =$ ____

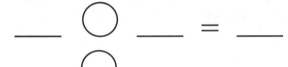

7-14 Estimate Time

Student textbook pages

See pp. 265–266.

Draw the time.

1. We eat at 5:30.   We finish at 6:30.

_____ to _____ is ____ hour.

Find the difference. Ring the ● being taken away.

See pp. 165–166.

Algebra ✓ 2.

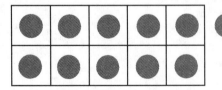   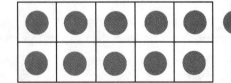

$11 - 8 =$ ____ $11 - 3 =$ ____

52

7-15 Calendar

Student textbook pages

See pp. 267–268.

Ring about how long.

1. cooking a pizza

about 1 minute

about 1 hour

Write the number that comes between.

See pp. 215–216.

2.   Between

before   after

63,   ___,   65

49,   ___,   51

97,   ___,   99

3.   Between

before   after

30,   ___,   32

76,   ___,   78

55,   ___,   57

Add or subtract.

See p. 102.

4.
$$\begin{array}{cc} 6 \\ +0 \\ \hline \end{array} \quad \begin{array}{cc} 5 \\ -5 \\ \hline \end{array} \quad \begin{array}{cc} 0 \\ +4 \\ \hline \end{array} \quad \begin{array}{cc} 3 \\ +0 \\ \hline \end{array} \quad \begin{array}{cc} 2 \\ -0 \\ \hline \end{array} \quad \begin{array}{cc} 2 \\ +0 \\ \hline \end{array}$$

Compare. Ring < or >.

See pp. 217–218.

Algebra 5.

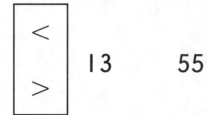

24   < >   42   31   < >   13   55   < >   45

Student textbook pages

Complete.

See pp. 269–270.

September

Sunday	Monday	Tuesday	Wednesday	Thursday	Friday	Saturday
					1	2
3	4	5	6	7	8	9
10	11	12	13	14	15	16
17	18	19	20	21	22	23
24	25	26	27	28	29	30

1. September has _____ days and _____ full weeks.

Ring about how long.

See pp. 267–268.

2. playing baseball

about 1 minute

about 1 hour

Count by 2s. Write how many in all.

See pp. 221–222.

3.

_____   _____   _____   _____   _____

_____ in all

Name _____   Date _____

Student textbook pages

See pp. 271–272.

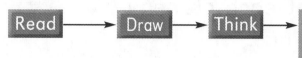

Read → Draw → Think → Which time makes sense? → Ring

1. Wash dishes

7:00

Finished at

11:00

7:30

Draw to make pairs and leftovers.
Ring odd or even.

See p. 46.

2.   **5** ●

Pairs	Left Over

odd

even

3.   **6** ●

Pairs	Left Over

odd

even

Student textbook pages

See pp. 285–286.

Draw lines to close each open figure.

1.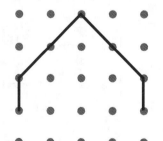

2.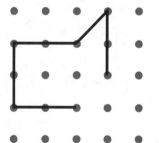

3.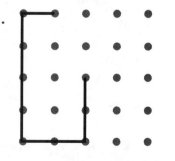

Write the place value and number.

See pp. 203–204.

4. thirty-seven _____

_____ tens _____ ones

5.   sixteen _____

_____ ten _____ ones

Student textbook pages

See pp. 287–288.

8-3 **Place-Value Chart**

Trace each side. Draw a ● at each corner.
Write how many each figure has.

1. 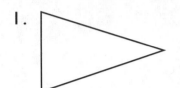 ___ sides

___ corners

2. 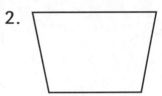 ___ sides

___ corners

Find the sum. Ring the numbers you add first.

See pp. 135–136.

Algebra ✓ 3. 5 + 2 + 2 = ___   4. 4 + 6 + 0 = ___

___ + ___ = ___   ___ + ___ = ___

8-4 **Same Shape**

Student textbook pages

See p. 289.

Ring three figures that have the same shape.
Write the name of the shape.

1.    _____

Trace each side. Draw a ● at each corner.
Write how many each figure has.

See pp. 287–288.

2. 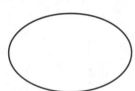 ___ sides

___ corners

3.  ___ sides

___ corners

Find the pattern. Write the missing numbers.

See pp. 211–212.

Algebra ✓

4. 50, 52, 54, ___, ___

5. 77, 76, 75, ___, ___

8-5 Same Shape, Same Size

Student textbook pages
See p. 292.

Trace each figure. Ring the same shape.

1.

2.

3.

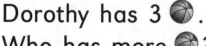

See pp. 179–180.

Algebra ✓ 4. Kora has 7 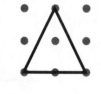.
Dorothy has 3 .
Who has more ?
How many more?

Kora |
Dorothy |

Who has more ?   Kora   Dorothy

___ − ___ = ___ ___ has ___ more .

8-6 Symmetry

Student textbook pages
See pp. 293–294.

Draw a figure with the same shape and size.
Describe and name each.

1.

Each has

___ sides ___ corners.

_____

Ring the amount.

See pp. 249–250.

2. 35¢

8-7 **Slides and Turns**

Student textbook pages

See pp. 295–296.

8-7 Slides and Turns

Ring the figures that show matching parts.

1.

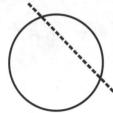 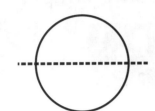 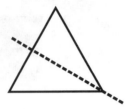 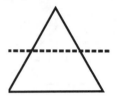

Draw the time that comes next.

See pp. 263–264.

Algebra ✓ 2.

half past ___   ___ o'clock   ___ minutes

after ___

8-8 Solid Figures

Student textbook pages

See p. 297.

Draw what is next. Ring slide or turn.

1.

slide

or

turn

Subtract. Check by adding.

See pp. 175–176.

Algebra ✓ 2. $12 - 7 =$ ___ $5 + 7 =$ ___

$11 - 3 =$ ___   ___ $+$ ___ $=$ ___

$7 - 5 =$ ___   ___ $+$ ___ $=$ ___

8-9 Cube, Pyramid, Rectangular Prism

Student textbook pages

See p. 298.

Ring the solids that roll.

1.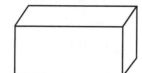

Ring three figures that have the same shape.
Write the name of the shape.

See pp. 289–290.

2.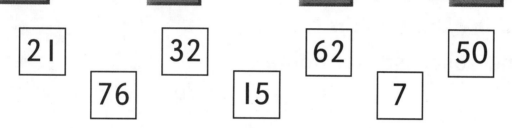

_____

| Read | → | Think | → | Write | → | Check |

See pp. 231–232.

Algebra ✓

| 21 | | 32 | | 62 | | 50 |
| | 76 | | 15 | | 7 | |

3. I am an even number greater
than 40 but less than 60.
What number am I?

Which numbers in the ☐ are even?

____ , ____ , ____ , ____

Which of these are greater than 40? ____ , ____ , ____

Which is less than 60? ____

Student textbook pages

See pp. 299–300.

8-10 Cylinders, Cones, Sphere

Match the solid with its name.

1.

pyramid

cube

rectangular prism

See p. 292.

Trace each figure. Ring the same shape.

2.   3.   4. ◯

See pp. 171–172.

Subtract. Complete the pattern.

Algebra ✓

5. $6 - 2 =$ ___ $5 - 2 =$ ___ $4 - 2 =$ ___

8-11 Making Bar Graphs

Student textbook pages

See pp. 301–302.

Match the solid with its name.

1.

cylinder

sphere

cone

See pp. 77–78.

Make a pictograph. Draw a △ for each tally.

2. III

 II

 ⵌ

Kind	Favorite Toy

See pp. 219–220.

Count by 5s. Write the missing numbers.

Algebra ✓

3. ___, 45, ___, 55, ___, ___, 70, ___, 80

8-12 Equal Parts

Student textbook pages

1. Color one box for each side.

Sides of Plane Figures

See pp. 303–304.

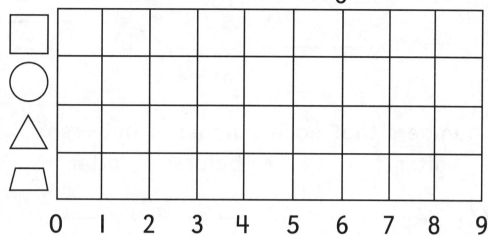

```
0   1   2   3   4   5   6   7   8   9
```

Make equal groups. Write the missing numbers. See pp. 223–224.

2.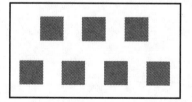

3.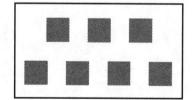

____ groups of 4 = ____   ____ groups of 3 = ____

____ fours = ____   ____ threes = ____

Subtract. Tell how many are left. See pp. 157–158.

4.

$7 - 5 = $ ____

5.

$7 - 2 = $ ____

8-12 Equal Parts

8-13 One Half

Student textbook pages

See pp. 305–306.

Write how many equal parts.

1. 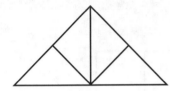   2. 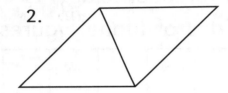   3.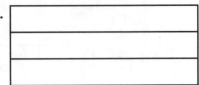

__   __   __

Write the numbers that each number is between.   See p. 215.

4. before   after

__, 97, __

__, 85, __

5. before   after

__, 52, __

__, 39, __

8-14 One Third

Student textbook pages

See pp. 307–308.

Ring the shapes that are $\frac{1}{2}$ shaded.

1. 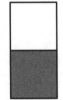   2.   3.

Add. Look for the pattern.   See pp. 131–132.
Write the next addition sentence.

Algebra 4.

6	7	8	9	
+2	+2	+2	+2	+

8-15 One Fourth

Ring each shape that shows $\frac{1}{3}$ shaded.

Student textbook pages
See pp. 309–310.

1.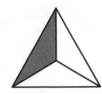

2.

3.

Ring to show equal groups.
Write how many groups.

See pp. 227–228.

4. 12 pennies in all.
3 in each group.

_____ = _____ groups of three.

Ring the amount.

See pp. 245–246.

5. 12¢

8-16 Part of a Set

Ring each shape that shows $\frac{1}{4}$ shaded.

Student textbook pages
See pp. 311–312.

1.

2.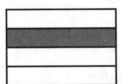

3.

Write how many equal parts.

See pp. 305–306.

4. 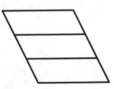 ____

5. ____

6. 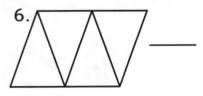 ____

Write the number that comes just before.

See p. 214.

7. ____, 36, 37   8. ____, 18, 19   9. ____, 69, 70

8-17 Always, Sometimes, Never

Student textbook pages

See pp. 313–314.

What part is shaded? Ring.

1.

$\frac{1}{2}$ $\frac{1}{3}$ $\frac{1}{4}$

2.

$\frac{1}{2}$ $\frac{1}{3}$ $\frac{1}{4}$

Draw to make pairs and leftovers.
Ring odd or even.

See p. 46.

3. **7** ●

Pairs	Left Over

odd

even

4. **8** ●

Pairs	Left Over

odd

even

8-18 Arrangement

Student textbook pages

See pp. 315–316.

Pick a marble from the correct bowl.

1. Ring always a ⬤. ✔ sometimes a ◯.

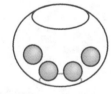   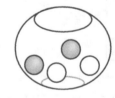

Write the amount. Match.

See pp. 255–256.

2.   _____ ¢

  **21¢**

3.   _____ ¢

  **11¢**

8-19 More or Less Likely

Student textbook pages

See pp. 317–318.

Draw ● or ○ on top of each shape
to make different designs.

1. You have  and ⬡.
   You have ● and ○.

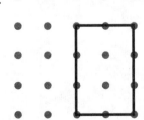

Compare. Ring < or >.

See pp. 217–218.

Algebra ✓ 2.

91 [< / >] 69   36 [< / >] 63   17 [< / >] 19

Show how you count on to add. Write the sum.

See pp. 129–130.

3. 6 + 6 = ___

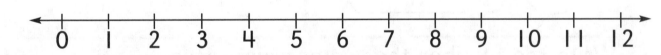

0 1 2 3 4 5 6 7 8 9 10 11 12

Draw a line to make matching parts.

See pp. 295–296.

4.

5.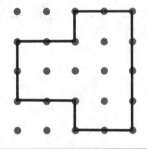

Algebra ✓ Put these numbers in order.

See pp. 209–210.

6. ___, ___, ___, ___, ___   70 67 62 64 69

Student textbook pages

See pp. 319–320.

Ring the correct answer.

1. Which color is the spinner most likely to land on?

black   gray   white

Trace each side. Draw a ○ at each corner.
Write how many each figure has.

See pp. 287–288.

2. 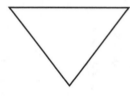   ___ sides

   ___ corners

3.    ___ sides

   ___ corners

Ring the solids that slide.

See p. 298.

4.

Write the number that comes just after.

See p. 213.

5. 42, 43, ___   6. 20, 21, ___   7. 95, 96, ___

9-1 Estimate About How Many

Student textbook pages

See pp. 323–324.

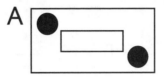 Read → Think → Write → Check

Which flag has:

1. 3 sides and 3 corners; and 1 circle and 2 rectangles inside?

   A   B   C   D

See pp. 169–170.

Subtract. Show how you count back.

2. $11 - 7 = $ ___

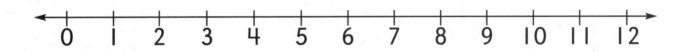

9-2 Add Tens

Student textbook pages

See pp. 335–336.

About how many ● are there? Ring.

1. 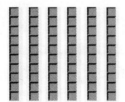   20   30   40

See pp. 197–198.

Write how many tens.
Write the number and the number word.

2. ___ tens ___

   _____

3. ___ tens ___

   _____

See pp. 195–196.

Write the missing number.

4. 12, 13, 14, ___   5. 7, 8, 9, ___

9-3 **Subtract Tens**

Student textbook pages

See p. 337.

Add.

1. 20 + 30 = ___

   2 tens + 3 tens = ___ tens

Subtract.
See pp. 165–166.

2.
11	9	7	8	11	6
− 2	−3	−5	−7	− 6	− 1

Write how many equal parts.
See pp. 305–306.

3. ___   4. ___   5. 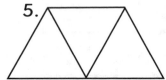 ___

9-4 **Add and Subtract Tens**

Student textbook pages

See p. 338.

Find the difference.

1. 9 tens − 7 tens = ___ tens

   90 − 70 = ___

2. 5 tens − 2 tens = ___ tens

   50 − 20 = ___

Match the solid with its name.
See pp. 301–302.

3.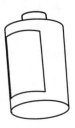

cylinder

sphere

cone

Name _____ Date _____

9-5   **Add Tens and Ones**

Student textbook pages

Add or subtract.

See pp. 339–340.

1.

$$
\begin{array}{r} 20¢ \\ +60¢ \\ \hline \end{array}
\qquad
\begin{array}{r} 30¢ \\ +10¢ \\ \hline \end{array}
\qquad
\begin{array}{r} 20¢ \\ +20¢ \\ \hline \end{array}
\qquad
\begin{array}{r} 10 \\ +50 \\ \hline \end{array}
\qquad
\begin{array}{r} 50 \\ +40 \\ \hline \end{array}
$$

2.

$$
\begin{array}{r} 80¢ \\ -60¢ \\ \hline \end{array}
\qquad
\begin{array}{r} 70¢ \\ -40¢ \\ \hline \end{array}
\qquad
\begin{array}{r} 20¢ \\ -10¢ \\ \hline \end{array}
\qquad
\begin{array}{r} 50 \\ -30 \\ \hline \end{array}
\qquad
\begin{array}{r} 80 \\ -40 \\ \hline \end{array}
$$

Draw the missing hand. Write the time.

See pp. 261–262.

3.

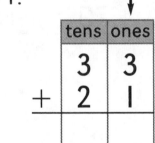

half past 4

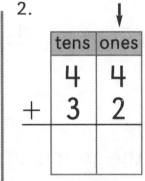

9-6   **More Adding Tens and Ones**

Student textbook pages

Add. First add ones.

See pp. 341–342.

1.

2.

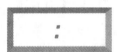

Write how many.

See pp. 199–200.

3.

tens	ones

_____ tens _____ ones

Add Tens or Ones

Student textbook pages
See pp. 343–344.

Add.

1.
```
  12      76      35      61      33      20
 +25     +13     +40     +16     +35     +29
```

Find the pattern. Write the missing numbers.

See pp. 211–212.

2. 34, 44, 54, ___, ___   3. 87, 85, 83, ___, ___

Draw the hour hand. Show the time.

See pp. 259–260.

4.
   5 o'clock

5.
   7:00

9-8 **Subtract Tens and Ones**

Student textbook pages
See pp. 345–346.

Add.

1.
```
  12      76      35      42      21      20
 + 5     + 3     + 2     +30     +70     +17
```

Draw the time.

See pp. 265–266.

2. We begin the game at 4:30. We finish at 5:30.

_____ to _____ is ___ hour.

9-9 More Subtracting Tens and Ones

Student textbook pages
See pp. 347–348.

Ring the ▭▭▭▭ and ▪ you subtract.
Write the difference.

1.

tens	ones
3	5
− 2	2

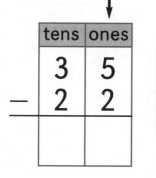

2.

tens	ones
2	8
− 1	6

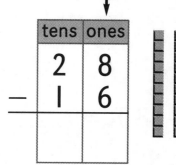

Subtract. Check by adding.

See pp. 175–176.

Algebra ✓ 3.

$$7 \atop -2$$ + $$9 \atop -3$$ + $$8 \atop -7$$ +

Write how much.

See p. 243.

4.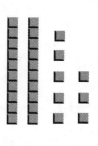

_____ nickels = _____ ¢

9-10 Subtract Tens or Ones

Student textbook pages
See pp. 349–350.

Subtract.

1. $$75 \atop -22$$ $$57 \atop -15$$ $$36 \atop -33$$ $$45 \atop -24$$ $$68 \atop -31$$ $$49 \atop -19$$

Count on. Write the amount.

See pp. 247–248.

2.

_____ ¢

Student textbook pages

Subtract.

See p. 351.

1.
$$
\begin{array}{r} 75 \\ -\ 3 \\ \hline \end{array}
\qquad
\begin{array}{r} 57 \\ -\ 5 \\ \hline \end{array}
\qquad
\begin{array}{r} 36 \\ -\ 2 \\ \hline \end{array}
\qquad
\begin{array}{r} 45 \\ -20 \\ \hline \end{array}
\qquad
\begin{array}{r} 68 \\ -10 \\ \hline \end{array}
\qquad
\begin{array}{r} 49 \\ -40 \\ \hline \end{array}
$$

Add.

See p. 337.

2. $40 + 30 =$ _____

4 tens + 3 tens = _____ tens

Add. Ring sums less than 9.

See pp. 121–122.

3. $3 + 6 =$ _____ $5 + 3 =$ _____ $1 + 8 =$ _____

Student textbook pages

Estimate the answer. Use a  .

See p. 354.

1. $34 + 37$ is about _____.

2. $38 - 32$ is about _____.

Write how much.

See pp. 251–252.

3.   _____¢

Ring each shape that shows $\frac{1}{3}$ shaded.

See pp. 309–310.

4.   5. 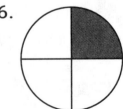   6.

72

9-13 Subtract Money

Student textbook pages
See pp. 355–356.

Find the sum.

1.
$$19¢ \qquad 38¢ \qquad 64¢ \qquad 36¢$$
$$+20¢ \qquad +41¢ \qquad +14¢ \qquad +21¢$$

See pp. 271–272.

2. Lunch 12 o'clock   Finished at

9-14 Using Addition and Subtraction

Student textbook pages
See pp. 357–358.

Find the difference.

1.
$$35¢ \qquad 56¢ \qquad 38¢ \qquad 64¢ \qquad 42¢$$
$$-20¢ \qquad -23¢ \qquad -11¢ \qquad -44¢ \qquad -31¢$$

Trade. Complete the table.

See p. 257.

2. Erin | ____ ____

Carlos | ____ ____

Carlos needs ____ _____.

9-15 Regroup in Addition

Student textbook pages
See pp. 359–360.

Ring the part you do first.
Add or subtract mentally.

Algebra ✓ 1. 75 − 10 + 2 = ___

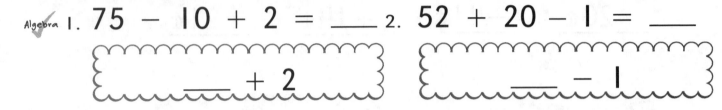

___ + 2

2. 52 + 20 − 1 = ___

___ − 1

See pp. 209–210.

Complete the place value. Color the number.

3. sixty-four ones

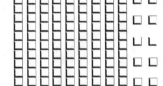

___ ones = ___ tens ___ ones

Subtract.

See pp. 163–164.

4. 10 − 5 = ___   9 − 8 = ___   10 − 3 = ___

9-16 Regroup in Subtraction

Student textbook pages
See pp. 361–362.

Add the ones. Regroup when you can.

1.

tens	ones

6 tens 8 ones + 3 ones

6 tens ___ ones = ___

___ tens ___ one = ___

Ring each shape that shows $\frac{1}{4}$ shaded.

See pp. 311–312.

2.

3.

4.

Name _____ Date _____

9-17 Problem Solving: Logical Reasoning

Student textbook pages

See pp. 363–364.

Subtract after you regroup.

1. 5 tens 1 one − 8 ones = 4 tens ____ ones − 8 ones

tens	ones

= ____ tens ____ ones

Read → Think → Write → Check

See pp. 323–324.

Which flag has:

2. 4 sides and 4 corners;
and 1 circle and
2 rectangles inside?

A   B   C   D

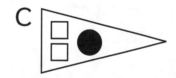

Draw a figure with the same shape and size.
Describe and name each.

See pp. 293–294.

3.    Each has

____ sides

____ corners.

_____

Write how much.

See p. 244.

4.

7 dimes = ____ ¢

10-1 Estimate and Measure

Student textbook pages

See pp. 365–366.

First write how much money each bank has.
Then solve using logical reasoning.

Bank A _____ ¢

1. It has less than 50¢.
   It has only 1 penny.

   A   B

   Bank _____ has _____ ¢.

2. It has more than 10¢.
   It has no quarters.

   A   B

   Bank _____ has _____ ¢.

Bank B _____ ¢

See p. 243.

3. Ring the amount.

   25¢

10-2 Perimeter

Student textbook pages

See pp. 379–380.

1. Estimate about how many ⬚.

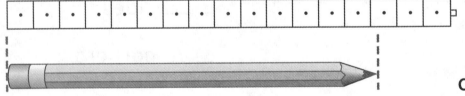

about _____ ⬚

See pp. 307–308.

Make equal parts. Color $\frac{1}{2}$.

2.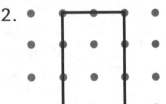

3.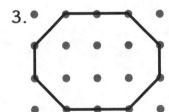

10-3 Inches

Student textbook pages

See pp. 381–382.

About how many  around each?

1.

about ____

2.

about ____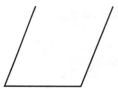

3. Draw what is next. Ring **slide** or **turn**.

See p. 297.

slide
or
turn

10-4 Feet

Student textbook pages

See pp. 383–384.

1. Use the _____. Measure the length.

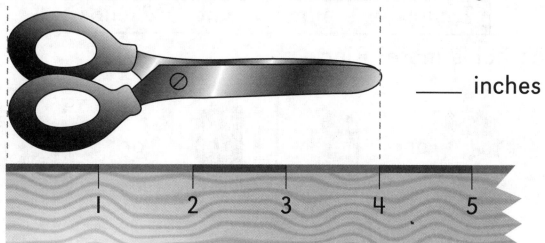

____ inches

2. Color each closed figure 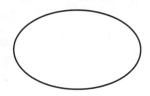 red.

See pp. 285–286.

10-5 Cups and Pints

Student textbook pages

See pp. 385–386.

Estimate the length of each real object.

1.

    more than 1 foot

    less than 1 foot

2.

    more than 1 foot

    less than 1 foot

Write how many.

See pp. 207–208.

3.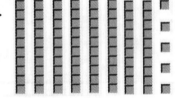

____ tens ____ ones

10-6 Quarts

Student textbook pages

See p. 387.

2 cups = 1 pint	1 pint = 2 cups

Which holds more? Ring.

1.    or

2.    or

Write each addend. Find the sum.

See pp. 341–342.

3.

tens	ones
+	

4.

tens	ones
+	

Name _____ Date _____

Student textbook pages

10-7 Pound

2 pints = 1 quart	1 quart = 2 pints

See p. 388.

Which holds more? Ring.

1.  or

2.  or

3. Write the amount. Match. See pp. 255–256.

32¢

28¢

_____ ¢   _____ ¢

10-8 Centimeters

Student textbook pages

1. ✔ about 1 pound. Ring less than 1 pound. See pp. 389–390.

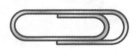

2. ✔ about 1 pound. Ring more than 1 pound.

3. Ring each cube. ✔ each rectangular prism. See pp. 299–300.

10-9 Using Centimeters

Student textbook pages

See pp. 391–392.

1. Use the . Measure the length.

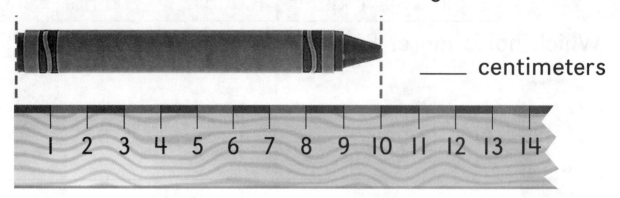

_____ centimeters

Ring the figures that show matching parts.

See pp. 295–296.

2. 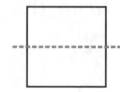   3.

10-10 Estimate a Liter

Student textbook pages

See p. 393.

1. Use the centimeter ruler.
   Ring the object if it is longer than 10 centimeters.

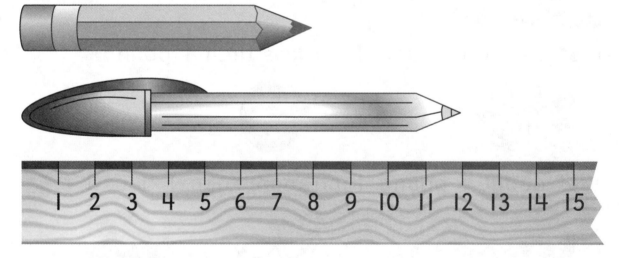

Color part of each set.

See pp. 313–314.

2. one half   3. one third   4. one fourth

      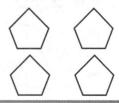

10-11 Kilogram

Student textbook pages

See pp. 395–396.

1. Ring more than 1 liter.

2. Color one box for each side.

See pp. 303–304.

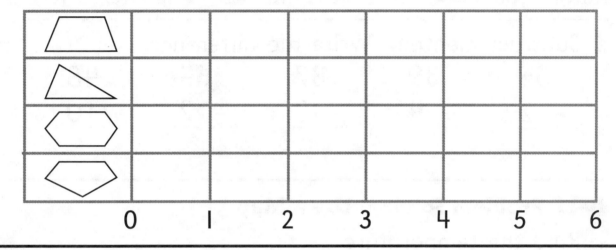

0   1   2   3   4   5   6

10-12 Measuring Tools

Student textbook pages

See pp. 397–398.

1. Which are less than 1 kilogram? Ring.

   red

10-13 Temperature

Student textbook pages

See p. 399.

Which tool would you use to measure each?

Ring C for .

Ring R for .

Ring B for .

1.

    C   R   B

2.

    C   R   B

3. Subtract mentally. Write the difference.

See p. 351.

56	39	87	64	48	95
− 2	− 4	− 3	− 2	−10	−20

10-15 Problem Solving: Use a Map

Student textbook pages

See p. 400.

1. Ring the temperature.
   Color the thermometer.

30°

70°

See pp. 319–320.

Color ◯ to show an equal chance
of picking red without looking.

2.

3.

Name _____ Date _____

11-1 Sums of 13 and 14

Student textbook pages

See pp. 403–404.

Solve. Use the map and these steps.

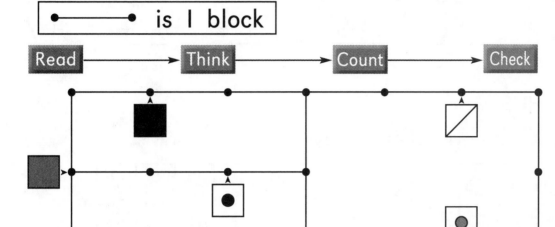

How far is it: 1. from ■ to ◻ ? _____ blocks

2. from ◻ to ◻ ? _____ blocks

3. from ▨ to ◻ ? _____ blocks

Write the doubles fact. Draw one more.
Write the new addition fact.

See pp. 133–134.

Algebra 4.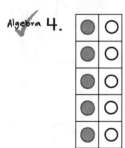

$$\begin{array}{r} 5 \\ +5 \end{array} \quad +$$

5.

$$+ \qquad +$$

Pick a marble from the correct bowl.

See pp. 315–316.

6. Ring always a ○. ✔ sometimes a ○.

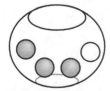  

11-2 Subtract from 13 and 14

Student textbook pages

See pp. 415–416.

Find the sum.

1.
$$\begin{array}{r} 8\cent \\ +5\cent \\ \hline \end{array}$$
$$\begin{array}{r} 6\cent \\ +5\cent \\ \hline \end{array}$$
$$\begin{array}{r} 4\cent \\ +9\cent \\ \hline \end{array}$$
$$\begin{array}{r} 8 \\ +4 \\ \hline \end{array}$$
$$\begin{array}{r} 8 \\ +4 \\ \hline \end{array}$$
$$\begin{array}{r} 6 \\ +7 \\ \hline \end{array}$$

See pp. 165–166.

Find the difference.
Ring the ⚪ being taken away.

 2.

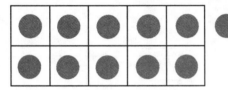

$11 - 7 = $ ___ $11 - 4 = $ ___

Find the difference.

See pp. 357–358.

3.
$$\begin{array}{r} 55\cent \\ -21\cent \\ \hline \end{array}$$
$$\begin{array}{r} 66\cent \\ -13\cent \\ \hline \end{array}$$
$$\begin{array}{r} 48\cent \\ -31\cent \\ \hline \end{array}$$
$$\begin{array}{r} 24\cent \\ -14\cent \\ \hline \end{array}$$
$$\begin{array}{r} 32\cent \\ -11\cent \\ \hline \end{array}$$

11-3 Sums of 15 and 16

Student textbook pages

See pp. 417–418.

Find the difference.

1.
$$\begin{array}{r} 11 \\ -8 \\ \hline \end{array}$$
$$\begin{array}{r} 13 \\ -9 \\ \hline \end{array}$$
$$\begin{array}{r} 12 \\ -6 \\ \hline \end{array}$$
$$\begin{array}{r} 14\cent \\ -9\cent \\ \hline \end{array}$$
$$\begin{array}{r} 12\cent \\ -9\cent \\ \hline \end{array}$$
$$\begin{array}{r} 14\cent \\ -8\cent \\ \hline \end{array}$$

Ring the part you do first.
Add or subtract mentally.

See p. 359.

Algebra ✓ 2. $27 + 20 - 4 = $ ___

___ $- 4$

11-4 Subtract from 15 and 16

Student textbook pages
See pp. 419–420.

Add.

1.
$$\begin{array}{r} 7 \\ +8 \\ \hline \end{array}$$
$$\begin{array}{r} 6 \\ +7 \\ \hline \end{array}$$
$$\begin{array}{r} 9 \\ +7 \\ \hline \end{array}$$
$$\begin{array}{r} 6 \\ +9 \\ \hline \end{array}$$
$$\begin{array}{r} 7 \\ +5 \\ \hline \end{array}$$
$$\begin{array}{r} 8 \\ +8 \\ \hline \end{array}$$

Draw ● or ○ on top of each shape to make different designs.

See pp. 317–318.

2. You have △ and ▽. You have ● and ○.

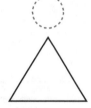

11-5 Facts of 17 and 18

Student textbook pages
See pp. 421–422.

Find the difference.

1.
$$\begin{array}{r} 16 \\ -\ 9 \\ \hline \end{array}$$
$$\begin{array}{r} 14 \\ -\ 8 \\ \hline \end{array}$$
$$\begin{array}{r} 16 \\ -\ 8 \\ \hline \end{array}$$
$$\begin{array}{r} 15 \\ -\ 7 \\ \hline \end{array}$$
$$\begin{array}{r} 15 \\ -\ 9 \\ \hline \end{array}$$

Algebra ✓ 2. Write other names for 12.

See pp. 155–156.

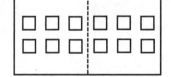
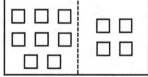
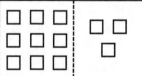

6 + 6 = ___ + ___ = ___ + ___ = ___ + ___

Find the difference.

See p. 338.

3. 9 tens − 4 tens = _____ tens   4. 6 tens − 3 tens = _____ tens

90 − 40 = ___   60 − 30 = ___

11-6 Fact Families

Student textbook pages
See pp. 423–424.

Find the sum.

1. 8 + 9 = ___   9 + 7 = ___   9 + 9 = ___

Write the fact family.

See pp. 177–178.

Algebra ✓ 2.

6 + 2 = ___   ___ ◯ ___ = ___

___ ◯ ___ = ___   ___ ◯ ___ = ___

Add.

See p. 337.

3. 40 + 40 = ___   4. 10 + 60 = ___

4 tens + 4 tens = ___ tens   1 ten + 6 tens = ___ tens

11-7 Three Addends

Student textbook pages
See p. 425.

Write the fact family.

Algebra ✓ 1. | 8 | 15 | 7 |

8 + 7 = ___   ___ + ___ = ___

___ − ___ = ___   ___ − ___ = ___

Add.

See pp. 135–136.

Algebra ✓ 2.
```
   4        2        3        1        6
   1        6        3        7        0
 + 2      + 4      + 5      + 2      + 3
```

Estimate the answer. Use the ⟵┼┼┼⟶.

See p. 354.

⟵——┼——┼——┼——┼——┼——┼——┼——┼——┼——┼——┼——⟶
   40 41 42 43 44 45 46 47 48 49 50

3. 43 + 49 is about ___.   4. 48 − 41 is about ___.

Name _____ Date _____

11-8 Problem Solving: Extra Information

Student textbook pages
See pp. 427–428.

Add up or down. Ring the group you use.

Algebra ✓ 1.

6	6	7	4	3
7	6	8	5	6
+3	+3	+2	+2	+8

Complete.

See pp. 269–270.

October

Sunday	Monday	Tuesday	Wednesday	Thursday	Friday	Saturday
1	2	3	4	5	6	7
8	9	10	11	12	13	14
15	16	17	18	19	20	21
22	23	24	25	26	27	28
29	30	31				

2. October has ____ days and ____ full weeks.

3. October has ____ Tuesdays and ____ Fridays.

4. The third Wednesday is October _____.

5. November begins the day after October _____.

Find the sum.

See pp. 125–126.

6.

$3 + 8 =$ ____

7.

$8 + 3 =$ ____

Student textbook pages

See pp. 429–430.

Draw a line through the sentence
that you do not need.

1. Rosa saw 14 🐄.
   5 🐄 were sleeping.
   6 🐄 were eating.

   How many 🐄 were
   not eating?

The _____ sentence
is extra information.

_____ – _____ = _____

_____ 🐄 were not eating.

Add or subtract.

See p. 102.

2.
$$8 \atop -8$$ $$7 \atop -0$$ $$0 \atop +9$$ $$8 \atop -0$$ $$6 \atop +0$$

Solve using logical reasoning.
First write how much money each bank has.

See pp. 365–366.

3. It has less than 40¢.
   It has only 1 dime.

   A   B

   Bank ___ has ___¢.

Bank A ___¢

4. It has more than 35¢.
   It has only 1 nickel.

   A   B

   Bank ___ has ___¢.

Bank B ___¢

12-2 Number Sentence Balance

Student textbook pages

See p. 443.

Algebra ✓ 1. Write the number sentence for each.
Draw another domino and number sentence
for the same rule.

  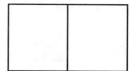

_____   _____   _____

Add mentally. Write the sum.

See pp. 345–346.

2.
$$53 \quad 76 \quad 82 \quad 64 \quad 30 \quad 29$$
$$+\ 4 \quad +\ 2 \quad +\ 7 \quad +20 \quad +12 \quad +30$$

12-3 Missing Operations

Student textbook pages

See p. 444.

Algebra ✓ Fill in the ☐. Solve to check.

1. $15 - 8 = \boxed{} + 3$ 2. $8 + 9 = \boxed{} + 7$

___ = ___   ___ = ___

Measure the length in inches.

See pp. 383–384.

3.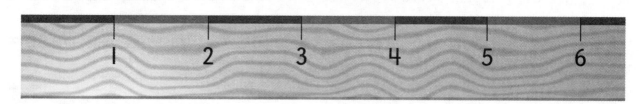

____ inches

12-4 Missing Numbers

Student textbook pages

See p. 445.

Algebra Fill in the missing signs.

1. 7 ◯ 5 ◯ 3 = 9   2. 11 ◯ 4 ◯ 5 = 2

Algebra 3. Find the missing numbers.

See pp. 339–340.

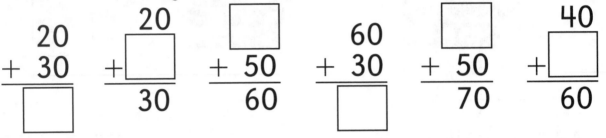

$$
\begin{array}{r} 20 \\ + 30 \\ \hline \square \end{array}
\qquad
\begin{array}{r} 20 \\ + \square \\ \hline 30 \end{array}
\qquad
\begin{array}{r} \square \\ + 50 \\ \hline 60 \end{array}
\qquad
\begin{array}{r} 60 \\ + 30 \\ \hline \square \end{array}
\qquad
\begin{array}{r} \square \\ + 50 \\ \hline 70 \end{array}
\qquad
\begin{array}{r} 40 \\ + \square \\ \hline 60 \end{array}
$$

12-5 Regrouping Money

Student textbook pages

See p. 446.

Find the missing number.

Algebra

1. ▱ = 37   ▱ – △ = 27   _____

△ = ?   ____ – △ = ____   △ = ____

Add the ones. Regroup when you can.

See pp. 361–362.

2. 4 tens 9 ones + 4 ones   3. 3 tens 7 ones + 5 ones

tens	ones

tens	ones

4 tens ____ ones = ____   3 tens ____ ones = ____

____ tens ____ ones = ____   ____ tens ____ ones = ____

4. Find the sum.

See pp. 355–356.

$$
\begin{array}{r} 33¢ \\ + 14¢ \\ \hline \end{array}
\qquad
\begin{array}{r} 54¢ \\ + 20¢ \\ \hline \end{array}
\qquad
\begin{array}{r} 26¢ \\ + 72¢ \\ \hline \end{array}
\qquad
\begin{array}{r} 45¢ \\ + 41¢ \\ \hline \end{array}
\qquad
\begin{array}{r} 30¢ \\ + 26¢ \\ \hline \end{array}
$$

12-6 Add Ones: Regroup

Student textbook pages
See pp. 447–448.

Find the sum.

1.

38¢	24¢	76¢	41¢	52¢
+ 7¢	+53¢	+ 8¢	+39¢	+19¢

Ring the heaviest. ✔ the lightest.

See pp. 389–390.

2.

12-7 Subtract Ones: Regroup

Student textbook pages
See pp. 449–450.

Write each addend. Add.

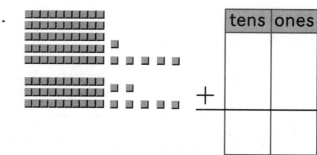

1. | tens | ones |
   |------|------|
   | | |
   | + | |

2. | tens | ones |
   |------|------|
   | | |
   | + | |

Subtract after you regroup.

See pp. 363–364.

3. 3 tens 1 one − 4 ones = ____ tens ____ ones − 4 ones

    = ____ tens ____ ones

tens	ones

Algebra ✔ 4. Find the sum. Change the order to check.

See pp. 343–344.

23		62		27	
+ 31	+	+ 17	+	+ 41	+

Student textbook pages

12-8 Three Addends: No Regrouping

Subtract. Ring to take away.

See pp. 451–452.

1.

tens	ones
5	3
−	7

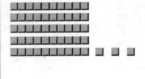

2.

tens	ones
6	1
−	5

Algebra ✓ Find the sum. Ring the numbers you add first.

See pp. 135–136.

3.
$$\begin{array}{r} 4 \\ 4 \\ +2 \\ \hline \end{array} \qquad \begin{array}{r} 2 \\ 3 \\ +4 \\ \hline \end{array} \qquad \begin{array}{r} 3 \\ 1 \\ +3 \\ \hline \end{array} \qquad \begin{array}{r} 6 \\ 2 \\ +1 \\ \hline \end{array} \qquad \begin{array}{r} 2 \\ 5 \\ +5 \\ \hline \end{array}$$

Find the sum.

See pp. 419–420, 423–424.

4. $9 + 6 = \underline{\quad}$ $9 + 9 = \underline{\quad}$ $8 + 9 = \underline{\quad}$

12-9 Hundreds, Tens, Ones

Student textbook pages

Find the sum.

See pp. 453–454.

1.
$$\begin{array}{r} 43 \\ 12 \\ +24 \\ \hline \end{array} \qquad \begin{array}{r} 62 \\ 23 \\ +11 \\ \hline \end{array} \qquad \begin{array}{r} 12 \\ 51 \\ +20 \\ \hline \end{array} \qquad \begin{array}{r} 22 \\ 31 \\ +14 \\ \hline \end{array} \qquad \begin{array}{r} 13 \\ 32 \\ +24 \\ \hline \end{array}$$

Which holds more? Ring.

See pp. 387–388.

2.  or

3.  or

Name _____ Date _____

12-10 Add and Subtract Three-Digit Numbers

Student textbook pages

Write the place value and the number word.

See pp. 455–456.

1.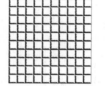

_____ hundreds _____ tens _____ ones

hundreds	tens	ones

_____

- -

_____

Ring the ⬜⬜⬜⬜ and ⬜ you subtract.
Write the difference.

See pp. 347–348.

2.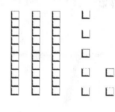

tens	ones
3	7
− 1	3

3.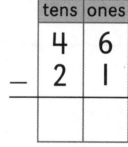

tens	ones
4	6
− 2	1

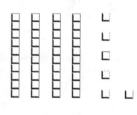

 Algebra Write the fact family.

See p. 425.

4. 8 5 13

___ + ___ = ___   ___ + ___ = ___

___ − ___ = ___   ___ − ___ = ___

5. 16 9 7

___ + ___ = ___   ___ + ___ = ___

___ − ___ = ___   ___ − ___ = ___

Student textbook pages

See pp. 457–458.

Find the sum.

1. 234 + 225

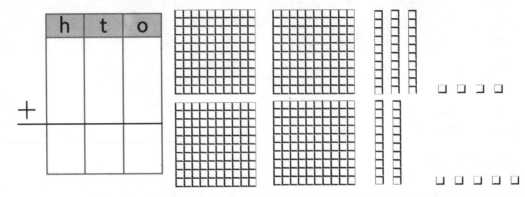

Algebra Add. Complete the pattern.

See p. 74.

2.

1	2	3	4	5	
+3	+3	+3	+	+	+

Solve. Use the map below. Use the shortest path. See pp. 403–404.

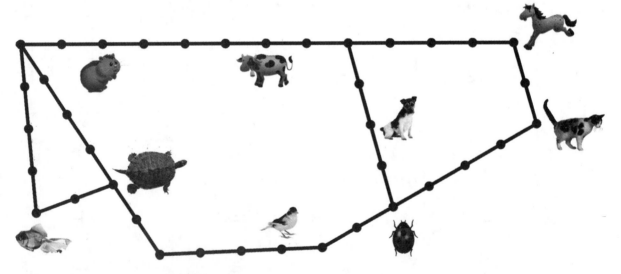

•——• is one unit

3. Go from the to the . ____ units

4. Go from the to the . ____ units